Samuel Osgood

Thomas Crawford and Art in America

Samuel Osgood

Thomas Crawford and Art in America

ISBN/EAN: 9783337395056

Printed in Europe, USA, Canada, Australia, Japan

Cover: Foto ©Thomas Meinert / pixelio.de

More available books at **www.hansebooks.com**

THOMAS CRAWFORD

AND

ART IN AMERICA.

Address before the New York Historical Society, upon the Reception of
Crawford's Statue of the Indian, presented by Frederic de Peyster,
LL.D., President, Tuesday Evening, April 6, 1875.

By SAMUEL OSGOOD, D.D., LL.D.

PUBLISHED BY ORDER OF THE SOCIETY.

NEW YORK:
JOHN F. TROW & SON, PRINTERS.
1875.

THOMAS CRAWFORD

ART IN AMERICA.

WE receive to-night the gift of a masterpiece from the chisel of the master sculptor of our America; and this fact, with its date, so full of interesting associations, tells us, that we Americans, as such, have something to do with the world of art. This month begins our round of Centennial jubilees; and whilst our Massachusetts neighbors are bent upon celebrating the battles of Lexington, Concord, and Bunker Hill, we may try our lungs a little at bragging in a different way, as we think not of smashing human profiles with muskets and cannon, bayonets and swords, but of modelling the human face as well as we can, in clay and marble, with hand and stick and chisel. Four hundred years ago, a month since, March 6, 1475, the prince of modern sculptors, Michael Angelo Buonarotti, was born, and we are just hearing the echo of the joy of Italy at the four hundredth anniversary of the birth of her illustrious son. This day, moreover, is the anniversary of the death of Raphael, who died April 6, 1520, three hundred and fifty-five years ago. Thus Italy, in the persons of her greatest sculptor and painter, meets with us now; and she who gave us Columbus and Americus, and who educated Crawford in his art, looks with a patronizing eye upon the rising art of our young America. It is nearly four hundred years since her Columbus opened our new world to the old; and there is something at first a little disheartening in the thought, that in all that time we have done nothing in art to equal her doings in the first hundred of those years, and that the first century since we became a nation has given us no name in sculpture or painting like those of Michael Angelo and Raphael.

But think a little more seriously upon the facts of the case, and there will be no occasion for discouragement. When Columbus, in April, 1492, fixed his articles of agreement with Ferdinand and Isabella for his great voyage of discovery, a Tuscan boy, who at fourteen had been apprenticed in 1489 for three years in the workshop of Domenico Ghirlandajo for about eight dollars a year, was practising his eye and hand among the busts, statues, and bas reliefs in the gardens of Lorenzo de Medici. Then, seventeen years old, he had shown his genius, and more than a year before, when under sixteen years, he had given immortality to a piece of marble by the touch of his chisel—the copy of the mask of the old Faun, which is still preserved in the public gallery of Florence. He lived to be nearly ninety years of age, and died February 17, 1564, about two months before William Shakespeare was born. There is something in this conjunction of names that honors the Italian sculptor, and also comforts us, the blood relations of the English poet. With all his marvellous genius and his manifold works as sculptor, painter, and architect, Michael Angelo never took hold of the popular life of Italy as Shakespeare took hold of England. He was obliged to give the gifts of his inspiration and the toils of his years to a power which he did not love, and instead of breathing a new spirit into dormant Italy, he helped to turn the influence of the rising revival of letters towards the restoration of mediæval despotism. Without meaning to do it, he helped to turn the Rome of Dante into the Rome of Loyola, and before he died he saw enough to tell him that the St. Peter's which rose under his master hand was not lifting the old Roman manhood, with the Roman Pantheon before the eyes of Italy, towards the mercy-seat of heaven.

Raphael, as he lay in state, robed for the grave, with his marvellous picture of the Transfiguration behind his head, this April 6, 1520, in Rome, the whole city doing him homage, was in more respects than one to be envied by his sublimer rival; for to Raphael beauty was its own paradise, and he opened its treasures to astonished Italy without any misgivings of the time when returning superstition would prefer the grotesque Bambino to his peerless Madonnas and Holy Child Christs, and the Barocco architecture of the Jesuit Church to the grandeur of Michael Angelo. Successful they both were, and their art was literature and eloquence to their time. Their pictures, statues, and buildings were poems, orations, romances, sermons, and philosophy, yet they

did not rise to the peculiar triumph which belongs
to the heroes of the new nations of Christendom,
and Thomas Crawford was happier than they in
having a great nation encourage his work and take
his art to fix its august memory and to exalt its majestic hope.

Michael Angelo's poems bring out the sadness of
which his life was full; and this generous Broad
Churchman, whose creed joined the thought of
Plato to the faith of St. John, felt that in the height
of his fame he was grinding, like Samson, in the mill
of the Philistines, and slaving himself to build up a
power which he little loved. This sonnet to Night
brings out the spirit of the man, and cheers our
America with promise of brighter day for her
Art :—

"O night! O sweet though sombre span of time!
        All things find rest upon their journey's end—
        Whoso hath praised thee well doth apprehend;
And whoso honors thee hath wisdom's prime.
Our cares thou canst to quietude sublime,
        For dews and darkness are of peace the friend;
        Often by thee in dreams upborne I wend
From earth to heaven, where yet I hope to climb.

Thou shade of Death, through whom the soul at length
        Shuns pain and sadness hostile to the heart,
        Where mourners find their last and sure relief,
Thou dost restore our suffering flesh to strength,
        Driest our tears, assuagest every smart,
        Purging the spirits of the pure from grief."

In this sonnet, and in his whole temper, there is
much of Michael Angelo that comes home to us all
now. A great achievement, his life was a great

prophecy, and was always suggesting more than he
did. His paintings and frescoes meant statues, and
his statues meant poems, and his poems breathed a
grand unrest, a perpetual sigh for the Renaissance,
the re-birth, that no beautiful arts nor priestly do-
minion, but the reign of God with mankind can se-
cure. Thomas Crawford's life, too, was full of
struggle, and it closed at forty-three years in shadows
dark in pain and disappointment without his fault;
but he was working towards the light, and the statue
of America on his country's Capitol holds out to
Italy a fairer promise than Michael Angelo ever
saw in the Basilica that sacrificed his country to a
caste. In the age of Leo X. the arts flourished at
the expense of liberty, humanity, and the highest
intellectual culture. There was too much and too
precocious blossoming for the best fruit. Literature
languished, that the arts of design might thrive.
Why lament, then, that our America has not suffered
thus, poor as she has been in the treasures of art!
Rather see the order of Providence in the destiny
that has allowed the sturdy trunk of our civilization
to grow for centuries here, and now at last the
promised bloom of beauty is to come without sacri-
fice of wisdom and strength. The hand that was
raised up to set the figure of Washington upon the
stately monument at Richmond cannot envy Michael
Angelo the tomb of the Medici and the mythical
shapes thereon. Washington and Cavour, practical
and prosaic as they were, mean more good to mankind, and in the end deeper inspiration to high art,
than all the Medici combined. In Italy superstition

used art to keep down the human mind, and made
Raphael put it to sleep by the charm of his beauty,
and Michael Angelo, in spite of himself, to frown
down its liberty by the grandeur of his genius. It
was worse in France, where the modern spirit was
laughed down by the fun of Rabelais and scared
away by the gloom of Calvin.

Times have changed now, and art, especially sculpture, has become the ally of liberty, the champion
of all generous culture. The spirit of Michael Angelo has gone, where it always belonged, to the free
mind of the northern nations, and Thomas Crawford
was one of his disciples; loyal member of that noble
brotherhood of sculptors, among whom Thorwaldsen was father, and Rauch and Drake and Schwanthaler and Dannecker were brothers. It devolves
upon me to speak of him to-night in connection with
art in America, and I must be allowed to say that
this office is not of my seeking, and did not seem to
belong to me; for I am not an artist, nor a critic, nor
a connoisseur, nor in any way qualified to teach the
principles or interpret the examples of art. I have a
certain love for the beautiful arts, and more love for
the ideal and harmonizing culture to which they belong; and perhaps it is not unbecoming in me, under
the circumstances, to appear here on this ground,
and, as a friend and helper of the higher education
of our people and their children, to speak of this
American sculptor and his beautiful art. A few
words of him, and then let us present the lesson of
his life.

I. The anniversary discourse before the society,

December 14, 1857, by Professor George W. Greene, was an eloquent tribute to the genius and character of Crawford. I had the honor of offering the resolution of thanks to the orator with some remarks. It is not for me, then, to undertake to do now what has already been done; yet I can properly recall enough of Crawford's career to place him distinctly before the minds of the young who did not hear that address, to say nothing of the elders, whose impression of it may have been obscured by the flight of years and the burdens of care. He was born in New York City, March 22, 1813, where he had a good common school education, and at the age of fourteen, after much study of drawing, with great attention to engravings and all works of art within his reach, he engaged himself to a wood-carver, with whom he remained till he was nineteen years of age, diversifying the work of carving wood with the study of architecture. At nineteen he entered the studio of Frazee & Launitz, monumental sculptors in this city, where he learned the mechanical part of sculpture and showed decided ability in modelling leaves, flowers, and other natural objects, and began to work upon portrait busts with success. In 1835 he started for Rome, and there, in Thorwaldsen, he met the presence and heard the words of encouragement that opened to him his destiny. Now twenty-two years of age, he had gone through his preparation, and his struggle began, which may be said to have ended with the reception of his statue of Orpheus in Boston, in 1841, and the happy marriage in 1844, which gave him, in a favored New York lady, the Eurydice

that he sought, without seeking her in any subterra-
nean shades. From that date to his early death,
thirteen years afterwards, his years of triumph were
counted. Great indeed were his labors for a young
man of forty-three years, the age at which he died,
and during his twenty years of professional life, with
only three visits home, in 1844, 1849, 1856, he finished
upwards of sixty works, many of them colossal, and
left about fifty sketches in plaster and designs of
various kinds. How impressive is the record of his
burial at St. John's Church in this city, where he had
always attended from his boyhood until he went to
Rome, and what changes have come since that day in
1857 when good Dr. Berrian read the burial service,
assisted by Rev. Messrs. Dix, Weston, and Young;
and Charles Sumner, Henry T. Tuckerman, George W.
Curtis, George W. Greene, Francis Lieber, and his
brother artists, Rossiter, Kensett and Hicks, were
pall-bearers. As we think of his death, at forty-three,
October 10, 1857, we may justly compare him with his
peers in art, and remember that Thorwaldsen died at
seventy-three, Canova at sixty-five, Bartolini at sev-
enty-two, Rauch at eighty, Dannecker at eighty-three,
Flaxman at seventy-one, Tenerani at over seventy.
Schwanthaler, who died at forty-six, after adorning
with colossal statues the throne-room of Munich and
the Walhalla of Ratisbon, and modelling the gigantic
statue of Bavaria, comes near to our American
sculptor in the originality and force of his genius, the
number of his productions, and in his early death.
But the Munich sculptor had a royal family to cheer
him, and the gold of a kingdom to support him and to

carry out his plans, whilst the American struggled for bread.

1. I will not undertake to describe or specify his works, but must be content with presenting the character of his genius and influence. And first of all he impersonated in himself the two essential qualities of the artist mind, the union of intense personality with the most generous and comprehensive universality. He was, from first to last, Thomas Crawford and nobody else, a marked and persistent individual, yet he grew out in all directions towards nature, humanity and God's providence. Although not a great scholar, familiar indeed with the French and Italian, and knowing the Greek and Latin classics only in translations, and never making any attempts at authorship, content with studying as well as he could the thoughts and style of the masters of literature, he was in his way a remarkable interpreter of the ages of history and the phases of human culture and genius from the days of Homer to those of Beethoven. As generally studied and written, history in its universal relations is dry and abstract, pedantic and unideal, but our sculptor made it live and speak in his creations. Its soul was embodied and its body was inspirited in every character that he studied and modelled. He could not of course do all that he aspired to do, and there are great gaps in his plastic rendering of the ages, but he evidently took them all within the sweep of his high and strong imagination and his tender and comprehensive humanity, and this New York wood-carver learned to accept and interpret the place of the nations in the order of

civilization; and broader and wiser than many a
learned commentator, he called up the characters of
Judea, Greece, Rome, Germany, America, to unfold
the apocalypse of time, to show the largeness of
humanity, and vindicate the providence of God.
What a rendering he has given of the American
Indian in the statue presented to us to-night. The
sculptor Gibson called it his finest work. What
strength and flexibility in the form; what majesty
and pathos in the expression; what rebuke in this
marble to us!

Intensely individual in his personality, and broad
and universal in his sympathy, he was able to
unite the two elements in his art and to present
the spirit of the ages in the speaking vitality of his
creations. This is perhaps the first essential of the
artist, that whatever he touches must have the breath
of personal life and the breadth of universal fellowship. The lonely little flower that blooms up from
under the shelter of an Alpine peak and catches the
gleam of sunshine among those icy banks, has its
own pertinacious organism, true in every tint and
fibre to the record and the banner of its clan; yet it
is one with universal nature, and when the painter
puts it upon canvas he brings out the catholicity of
its solitary confession and makes it tell its whispers
with the winds, its banquets with the dews and rains,
and its messages of love from the rocks of the earth
to the stars of heaven. Crawford had this power
in an art less free than the painter's, and under the
touch of his chisel the sheaf of California wheat
became personal, and its full blades were swelling

with the magnificence of the Pacific domain and even glowing with the gold of the mines that seemed to ask the grain to signal their hidden splendor to the world.

2. In one respect Crawford deserves honorable and conspicuous name among the leaders of our modern culture, and its master-spirit Goethe, would not have been ashamed to call him brother for what I call his next marked characteristic. He is one of the spirits of peace who are bringing the two great schools of civilization together—the classic school that insists most upon the body and form of things, and the romantic school, that insists most upon the soul and spirit of things—or the Greek and the Gothic. When Crawford begun his career these two powers were at war, as in fact they have generally been, but their antagonism was coming to a head. The Greek spirit was trying to set up again the rule of the body, and the age of industry combined with the restless muscle of the young nations to restore the dynasty of the legs and arms, and to set the gymnast above the philosopher and the devotee. This muscular creed was met by its ascetic antagonist, the Mediæval devotee; and Pugin's churches and Pusey's tracts made a dead set against the Turner's leg and club law and the secularists' whole code of culture. Thus it was Greek against Goth—body against soul. We saw the antagonism sometimes in buildings on opposite sides of the same street. Here a bank in not always cheap imitation of the Parthenon, and there a lath and plaster Gothic church in very cheap imitation of York Minster or Cologne Cathedral. These extreme contrasts marked schools of culture, not always extreme or

extravagant in their thought and enterprise, the
classic and the romantic. Goethe in his Faust called
for the end of this quarrel, and in Euphorion, the child
of the marriage of Faust with Helena, he predicted
the union of the classic and romantic schools in our
rising literature.

Now I do not say that Crawford cared much about
this literary quarrel, or meant to have his hand in the
fray, but I am sure that he felt the painful differ-
ence and was moved to do his part towards the true
reconciliation. He certainly did much towards the
result. His chief productions unite classic strength
with romantic spirituality. He is Greek and Gothic
or German too. He gives us the body and the soul
of man and nature. His first great work, his Orpheus,
is example of this union, and when I saw the noble
figure thirty-four years ago in Boston, it seemed to
me to settle the question that sculpture is a modern
art and allows the modern inward life to show itself
with the antique strength of form. Orpheus is a
Greek and a Christian too, and he faces toward the
the Shades or Erebus with limbs trained in the palæ-
stra and with a soul illuminated by the light that
is not of this world. This work is a prophecy of
our coming literature as well as art. It is one of the
signs of the new age of Germanic inwardness and
Greek outwardness. We are not to have muscle and
materialism on one hand and spindling pietism on the
other, but body and soul are to go together. Architecture and sculpture are not to be behind in the
reconciliation. Sculpture especially is to rebuke
alike the ghostly shadow and the fleshy materialism

that confront each other, and to show that personality requires soul and body; that within nature there is a mysterious life, and all in art should interpret the indwelling spirit and bring it out in fitting form. This thought is the key-note to our most characteristic and hopeful culture, and it throws bright light upon the new age now opening upon us. Crawford threw its radiance on every sphere of nature and life, and under his hand the wheat and the wild-flowers, playful children and merry youth, as well as heroic men, were transfigured by his touch.

3. We see its application to the institutions and life of our own nation to which Crawford has been a teacher and a prophet. The years of his artist work were critical years for our America, and he went to Rome after the first struggle with nullification had come to a head in its defeat, and the plans were in progress for the second struggle and final defeat. In 1835 our people were feeling, as never before, their place among the nations, and when he returned home to America in 1849, and received the orders for the Virginia monument of Washington, and for the colossal sculptures for the national Capitol, we had entered upon our cosmopolitan period and our imperial greatness, with the gold of California, the conquest of Mexico, the accession of new States at home and swarming fleets of ocean steamers abroad to make us proud of our position and to call for some conspicuous help from the hand of art to give America her true beauty before the world, and to lift her above the materialism that threatened her life. Crawford did the work nobly, and at Richmond and in Washington he set up

the nation in marble and bronze as eloquently and
bravely and persistently as Webster and Clay set it up
in speech, or Meade or Hancock or Thomas or Grant
ever set it up or kept it up by the sword. And he did
what they perhaps neglected; for he not only struck
his chisel against the conspirators who sought power,
but against the Mammon worshippers who were ready
to sell their country for money to the slave lords or
any other buyer. The sculptor was an inspired pa-
triot, and his chisel was pen and sword at once. He
modelled and carved the thought that was to rule the
land, and he put it upon the dome of the Capitol in
readiness for the great struggle that was to come.
The modern age is the age of the nations, and the
modern languages are their voice, the declaration of
their liberty and law, the pledge of their birthright
and their perpetuity. These languages speak not in
words alone but in deeds also, and sculpture puts
their great utterance into brass and marble. Thought-
ful, earnest men are doing this work now in every free
nation, and Crawford as no other man has done this
for us. Upon the bronze doors, upon the pediment
and the dome of the Capitol, he has embodied the
characteristic ideas and institutions of our country,
and his record has been read by the nation and told
its power in the homes and schools, the armies and
the Senate halls of the republic. He has recorded
not a spiteful clannishness or provincial jealousy or
aggressive sectionalism, but a broad and generous
nationality, with protection to every citizen, and
towards the whole world the blessing that he read in
his prayer-book, " unity, peace, and concord to all

nations." The body and the soul of the nation he
recognized, and he has done his part in keeping its
body and its soul together, the land with the law, the
soil with the people. There was power in that sculp-
tured record—power not wholly his own; for as there
is a mysterious life in nature, and whilst man plants
and waters, but the increase is from above and
within, so it is in history. A mighty spirit moves over
the ages, and all true and high souls are its oracles.
The Lord of Hosts, who raised up the Father of our
country, raised up the hand that carved his statue
and enthroned that country in majesty. It takes
the combined lessons and arts of all ages to make a
good work of art; and the America that looks down
upon us from the dome of the Capitol comes to us
from a hand not only trained in the schools of art,
but guided by the spirit that of old called order
from chaos, and is the Lord and Giver of life. Nothing is done well that is done in self-will without the
mysterious overruling will, and our sculptor's work,
like the workman, was proof that he bowed to that
power. Forces as well as ideas go with true art, and
the sculptor's chisel cuts the channels in which these
forces run, pouring as they do their tides of moral
power in characters that never fade. As beauty has
its point of bloom, and art puts it upon canvas to
bloom there always, so heroism has its point of fruit-
age, and the art that seizes this point and puts it
into stone or bronze, makes it tell the fact to all time,
whether in David's dashing bravery or Washington's
calm endurance. Thus interpreted, the America that
crowns the Capitol seized the rising national spirit of

2

the country as it moved the artist to the inmost being,
and there it stood when the fearful trial came for
the nation's life, and there it stands now, calling us to
move on to the century opening upon us now, strong
in the God of our fathers and with the transmitted
life of his people.

How much any one work or any one man can do
or has done it is not easy to calculate, but we must·
remember that the measure of the mass of weight or
force of motion is not by the sum total, but by the
balance of conflicting elements. He starts the ava·
lanche who overcomes the weight that keeps the
centre of gravity in poise, and he moves the nation
to its daring who overcomes the inertia that keeps
it from moving. The few monuments of patriotic
art that we had in our struggle gave their silent
force to the flag, and the majestic figures in our Union
Square and at the Capitol fought for us from first
to last, and brass and marble gave out the latent
fires in which their material was formed and their
proportions were shaped.

II. The lesson of Crawford's life to us, his coun-
trymen, cannot be easily misunderstood. It tells us
to accept the true idea of the art which he followed,
to carry it out in the education of our children, and
to make it tell upon the public spirit of the nation.

1. The true idea of art—what is that? There
have been definitions of art without number, but
they all amount to very much the same thing. Art
is the way to do things, and fine art is the way to do
things finely; the way to put soul into body, to lift
the actual to the ideal, to see and bring out the spirit

that is in nature and life, and to exalt the things
that are seen to the standard of the beauty that is
unseen. All depends upon following the method of
the Creator, and in accepting the two facts of soul
and body wisely and effectively. Without soul we
have clay and flesh and blood without life, and with-
out.body we have only notions, shadows, dreams so
far as present evidence can go. The point is to study
carefully the reality of things, and to express the
truth in the form of beauty, understanding by beauty
not prettiness or pleasantness merely, but whatever
belongs to the true harmony and unites the many
particulars with the supreme perfection. In this
sense art is not any one craft, whether architecture,
sculpture, painting, that use the hand and appeal to
the eye, nor poetry, music, oratory, that use the voice
and appeal to the ear; but it is all good work
that beautifies and exalts life, and raises nature and
man up to the ideal standard. There is fine art in
manners, in society, in influence over schools and
nations, in teachers and statesmen, in the pioneers of
civilization, and in the ministers of religion. Whatever sees the truth of things and works out their
possible beauty is of the essence of beautiful art.
The mother, who refines her home and moulds her
children and elevates her family and helps Chris-
tianize her neighborhood, is sister of the Muses, and
none of the Nine need be ashamed of her company.
The captain who subdues the reckless animalism
of his crew and wins them to order, gentleness,
loyalty, and reverence, is brother to the sculptor
who strikes intelligence into shape from the rough

marble by his touch, and makes it tell to all time its
lesson.

We need to accept this generous definition of art,
and to broaden its fellowship in order to show the
narrowness of the mere craftsmen who wrong beauty,
just as priestcraft wrongs religion, by claiming the
exclusive right to its spirituality. The artist, like
the preacher, needs to be one among men, not apart
from them, and the more he is a representative
brother and the less an official lord, so much the better for him and them. There is no danger that art,
any more than religion, will decline under this true
fellowship of souls. Taking this view we must be
willing to appreciate all attempts to adorn life and
to bring the supreme beauty to bear upon the world.
We must be willing to see the spirit of art where
its implements are poorly mastered, and to believe
that our stout fathers and frugal mothers were working America into shape before sculpture and painting
appeared; that many an Isaac carved the image of
his Rebecca out of the rough fortune with which he
struggled for her sake, and many a Jacob painted
his Rachel upon streams and clouds during his long
service for her hand, and made the picture solace him
by the way like a Madonna face at the stations
upon the pilgrim's path. In time the spirit of beauty
took more organic shape, and we had painters, sculptors, architects, as well as orators, poets, and singers
of our own. Perhaps free speech was the first of
our American fine arts in order of time, and the
eloquence of rising liberty brought the spirit of grace
earliest to our land. Before printing had made love

to painting here, and engraving was born of their marriage, a printer's boy began the arts of beauty, and Franklin's prose style had nothing to learn of the scholars of England or the wits of France.

When Crawford appeared we had no first-class sculpture, little good architecture, little painting of the high historical school. He made us strong where we expected to be most weak, and won to himself a name in an art that was supposed to belong to antiquity and to linger beyond its time upon the modern stage. He made us feel that it belongs to us and to our country. Why not, for what does sculpture mean but man and character, and where ought these to be more accepted than here, where we have not the rich costumes and brilliant courts that painting delights in, and if we have not men and characters we are poor indeed. Think of him, as he was bent upon his first attempts at sculpture here, in his years of service with Frazee & Launitz, and let the description in Professor Greene's words bring him and his art near to our American thought: "Most of his time the whole of his daylight belonged to his employers; but the evenings were his own, and how happy was he when the evening sunlight, slowly creeping up the wall, announced the approach of the hour that was to set him free; and when hurrying home for a hasty meal, he could take his notes under his arm and return to his studio for his evening labor of love. If, of the hundreds that hourly passed by that humble door in the pursuit of pleasure or gain, some curious one had stopped to look in, he would have seen a young man about five feet

eleven inches high, of a slight but vigorous frame,
with prominent eyes of clear blue, ample forehead,
lips full but firm, cheeks flushed with an excitement
that heightened the ruddy glow of health, the mus-
cles of the face already formed to the expression of
deep feeling and elevated thought, the thick chestnut
hair sprinkled with marble dust, a modelling tool in
his hand, and on the stand before him a head of
clay on which the light fell imperfectly from a can-
dle strongly fastened in his hat. He would have
seen that there was no common earnestness in that
face, no common skill in that hand; and oh! why,
of the hundreds revelling in superfluous wealth, could
not one have discovered in the toiling youth the
future author of the Orpheus, and, devoutly thank-
ing God for the privilege, held out a brother's hand
to help him in his hour of need, over the rugged pass
that still divided him from the full possession of his
powers!"

2. Such was Crawford, a youth of twenty-three;
and what he was in susceptibility thousands and tens
of thousands now in the land are, and some of these
not without sparks of his genius. How great, then,
the need of a better art education here for our children—an education not merely for those who are
to be artists by profession, but for all who have
any sense of beauty and any aspiration for refine-
ment in life. This education ought to be thorough-
going, to begin at the beginning of intelligence and
comprehend all faculties of our nature and all
fields of art. It should begin before books and
schools, and should bring all the intellectual and

active powers into direct contact with the world of beauty.

It is a fine remark of Saint Beuve that taste is the first essential of criticism, and when we judge a book, as when we eat an apple, it is more important to taste its quality well than to analyze its elements scientifically. According to this idea it is important to cultivate a living and just taste in our children, and this is to be done not by treatises on æsthetics, but by accustoming them to observe and to enjoy the best things for themselves. All the senses are to be properly trained, and instead of making children plod over books and cram their memories with words, they should be taught to touch, and hear and see nature and art for themselves. Object teaching should go before letter teaching, and it is perhaps best that they should have nothing to do with books and verbal lessons before they are seven years old. This is evidently the method of nature, and Froebel with his Kindergarten is the prophet of a good time coming for the emancipation of children from the yoke of the old pedagogues and of their admittance to the new liberty of nature and art. All the senses are to be educated in connection with their proper objects, and form, color, mass, perspective are to be known and interpreted in themselves, and not in lifeless print and prosy description. By wise selection and adaptation, all the senses may be developed into a true sense of the beautiful, and may open into a practical judgment that is not only the foundation of the critical faculty, but also an essential condition of all practical good sense.

We need, not only for professional artists, but for all well educated people, a certain judgment that cannot be looked for too early, and which in matters of taste holds the same place that conscience holds in the sphere of morals. It is as unwise to limit this judgment to artists and professional critics as to limit conscience or the religious sentiment to the clerical class or to ethical and theological writers; for just as all true men are called to have ethical and religious convictions, so all cultivated people are bound to have a due sense of the beautiful and fair judgment upon the best examples of beautiful art. This judgment, like the moral sense, depends more upon wholesome associations than upon theory, and when children are accustomed to see beautiful objects, to walk among flowers and birds, lawns and groves, by rivers and lakes, to look upon good pic- tures and statues, and to be among people of gentle speech and graceful manners, they catch the spirit of beauty, both as a sentiment and a conviction; and their pleasure in the taste, like the flavor of the strawberry and the peach, passes into the very con- stitution, and the sweetness on the lips is light in the brain and in its chambers of imagery. We want in all of our education more of that fine element in reason that feeds on the beautiful and transfigures its sweetness into light. Any one who has gone with bright children into the gardens or the art gal- leries and seen the quick intuitions that flash up from their ready perceptions, will discern at once what I mean by this intellectual influence of beauty, and he will not regard Edmund Spenser a dreamer for calling thus upon Heavenly Beautie in his Hymne :

"Cease, then, my tongue! and lend unto my mynd
    Leave to bethink how great that Beautie is,
Whose utmost parts so beautiful I find ;
    How much more those essential parts of His,
    His truth, His love, His wisdome, and His blis,
His grace, His doome, His mercy and His might,
By which He lends us of Himselfe a sight!"

There is of course another side to this art education—the more active side, for art is essentially active and its virtue is eminently in the sphere of the
will. This activity needs training alike in origin-
ating enthusiasm and executive power. Here is the
sad truth with the prevailing methods of education,
that they do not stir the will to enterprise or to
achievement, but content themselves too much with
impressions and words. Here too the common artistic culture has been too feeble, and passive taste
has taken the place of earnest aspiration and active
force. Why not begin with setting this matter
right? Why not put the spirit of originality into
our children by making them hunt out object lessons for themselves in the gardens and woods and by
the water? Little Billy can be trained to delight
more in bringing flowers, mosses, leaves, berries and
shells from his rambles than in robbing birds' nests,
and he and his companions, girls as well as boys, can
grow up with a well-spring of original life within
them, that will tell not only upon their own lot, but
upon the tastes of society, and in time interpret itself in gardens, halls, pictures, statues, music and

all gentle arts, whether by the patronage that encourages genius to do its work, or by the gifts of
genius itself in their persons. We want this fresh,
life-seeking, life-giving spirit everywhere to stir and
elevate our dull routine and our feeble and exacting
pleasure-seeking generation.

With this original freshness executive force should
go, and it is the essential characteristic of art that
it compels its disciple to work and never to be content with any dream of beauty apart from doing it
into artistic form. Here our sculptor is a noble example—a good mechanic as well as an imaginative
designer. He had learned to carve wood and marble before he moulded clay or pencilled sketches,
and his mechanical skill had much to do with his
artistic excellence. We all need to remember this
fact and to beware of the dreamy, bookish, imbecile
culture that stops with fine notions and never car-
ries the idea forth to the deed. We cannot do
without mechanical skill, and our artists sometimes
fall short of the true mark by being content with
the literary part of their art; calling themselves
architects and sculptors because they can dream of
buildings and statues with little power to put them
into wood and stone. My impression is, that the
best recent experience of art education leads us to respect more and more the example of such men as Al-
bert Dürer and Michael Angelo, who were mechanics as well as artists, and to urge the need of training our young artists in the strong and true hand
as well as in the quick brain and the fertile fancy.
Why not carry this principle into all education, and

put muscle as well as mind into all our schooling? Why not put away a great part of the verbiage and cramming from our schools, and teach even little children the alphabet of nature and the handwriting of art? Why not teach them to seek out and to see all the attributes of things for themselves, and to write them out with their own hand in characters of form, color, and mass? We ought all to learn to draw or paint or model, and if possible combine all these arts of expression, not to make us all artists, but to give us mastery over our own faculties and the nature of things. The leaders of education are seeing this need and meeting it. The deluge of print is abating, and as its waters subside we are seeing the green earth, the meadows, the trees, the birds, the cattle, and the farms and habitations of men, and asking power to render them in all their reality, instead of being content with pale shadows of them on the printed page. We need to reform education in both directions—to make muscle more artistic and to make art more muscular. Our modern division of labor is the result of the sectarian spirit that divides men by the very differences that ought to bring them together, and the separation of practical gifts, that need each other, is worse than the war of speculative opinions that have perhaps outlived their day. The workman needs to be again brother to the artist and to love the plan of the building on which he works. The artist needs to be again a workman and to carry ideal enthusiasm into the hammer as well as the pencil, and to put hand and heart into architecture and engineering. It is a pity that Italy did not appreciate Leonardo da Vinci and Michael Angelo as mechanics and engineers as well as painters and sculptors, and use their genius to bring health to the malarious marshes and work and competence to the impoverished people. This union of genius with industry must come, and the true artist must not only charm our leisure by his fancy, but he must invigorate and ennoble the life of nations by his skill and invention and enter-prise.

Carry out these ideas of art education, and our whole standard of culture rises, our boys and girls. will have better senses and judgment, aspirations and powers for their various spheres, whilst they who have especial ability as artists will be prepared for their vocation in the especial schools of art. All honor to these especial schools—to the Cooper In-stitute, to the Academy of Design, to the public schools of art which are now rising throughout Christendom and in which, so far as America is con-cerned, I believe the State of Massachusetts has taken the lead, not merely for the refining of the taste of her people, but for the elevation of her industry and the increase of her wealth.

3. In all this effort we need a broad and generous public spirit, and we are apparently to have it in due time. Our public spirit has not been hard or selfish, but it has been busied mainly with working the soil and our industry into shape and giving as far as possible the polish of grace to the implements of toil and the stamp of art to the structures of in-dustry and thrift. We need to know better than

we do, that labor languishes and thrift fails without
the true endowment of beauty ; that all capital is
not to be counted in money, and the peerless be-
quests of former generations, the masterpieces of
ages, are seen without money and enjoyed without
being exhausted.   What a blessing in the assurance
that so much has been done by gifted men that is
the lasting property of the human race, and that
the treasures of art, like the perfections of God, are
not wasted by being used, and the more they are
known and appreciated, the more they abound.
Happy therefore are they who give such gifts to the
people as our President has given to-night. The be-
quest shall live when he is gone and our children's ·
children have passed away.

The want of the art spirit and its products here
puts us at disadvantage in comparison with Europe,
and our people go abroad in part to escape the worry
and anxiety of this new and crude country, where
nothing is finished, to find relief in the old world
where centuries gather their treasures, and life has
something of the finish that makes it the Sunday of
grace and not the perpetual washing-day of scrub-
bing and discontent. The art spirit is to help us
out of this difficulty, and instead of robbing us of
our young energy, it is to open to it new visions of
triumph and to give our restless dash the calmness
which is the crown of true power, and without which
its force is a fever that ends in imbecility and death.
Let us have, then, our true art culture, and have it in
our own way in the interests of our liberty and order, in loyalty to the justice and humanity that we

acknowledge and in service of the religion that we revere.

There is no want of subjects for our artists, nor of genius for the arts. For more than a hundred years we had gifted men of our own stock who have shown conspicuous gifts, and surely nature is fair enough for our landscape painters, and our people and our history are not wanting in traits for the historical painter and the sculptor. Some of our best artists have been trained at home, and they have found scenes and figures enough for them here. Our men certainly are not bad looking, and our women are, to speak with moderation, as fair as any in the world—the fairest of any, we may perhaps safely say. If our art took its lead from Italy, it has in some respects rivalled its masters, and probably we have American sculptors and painters—sculptors surely, who surpass any contemporary Italians. They told me in Rome that there was but one Tenerani, and I looked into his atelier, alas! on the day after his death, earnest even at that time to pay my tribute to this gifted pupil of Thorwaldsen. But he evidently had been overpowered by the antique that he had so devotedly studied, and he had not, like Crawford, used its severe and massive form so as to help him to shape a higher ideal of humanity. It is well if our America can pay her debt to Italy in any way, and like the Roman daughter give back the tide of life to her parent. It is well that Michael Angelo finds here an interpreter that Rome has not allowed him to find at home, and whilst Rome sends to America the Cardinal's hat, America has antici-

pated the compliment by sending to her the liberty-
cap which Crawford there designed before he chis-
elled it on the head of his colossal statue. That
liberty-cap is something more than a compliment,
and with the cocked hat of the Continental army of
our American Revolution it has told and is telling
upon the public opinion of Europe and of Rome
more powerfully than any of the honors or the ful-
minations of the Vatican. Perhaps Italy is in this
respect changing places with America, and whilst
we are accepting her art, she is accepting our industry and thought, and doing last for her people
the work of health and thrift, which we did first—
making the rule of utility come after her empire of ·
beauty.

All honor and success to her in each sphere! Italy
and America—whom God hath joined together let
not man put asunder! This word for Italy it is
well to say on this four hundredth year since Michael
Angelo's birth, and to add these noble words of
Christopher Pearse Cranch :—

    " Ennobled by his hand
    Florence and Rome shall stand,
        Stamped with the signet ring
    He wore where kings obeyed
    The laws the artists made.
        Art was his world and he was Art's anointed king.

    " So stood this Angelo
    Four hundred years ago ;
        So gravely still he stands,
        'Mid lesser works of art,
        Colossal and apart,
        Like Memnon breathing songs across the desert sands."

Now that we are counting our first century of
national life, it is well for us to recollect ourselves
somewhat seriously, and in our letters and art try to
perpetuate the best lessons and examples of our
record. All art rests upon experience, and Memory,
mother of the Muses, gives the great subjects for
invention as for history. Crawford has done his
part to embody the great remembrances of our nation,
and we are asked to combine all true men and principles and powers to give continuity to his work.
Mere individualism cannot do anything great or
good, and all nobleness starts in a memory beyond
the individual man, and combines forces and con-
tinues influences beyond his egotism. It is well for
us to bring out the wealth of our record, to set the
images of our fathers in the front of honor, to rebuke
self-seeking and knavery in high places by the dig-
nity of august examples as well as by the majesty
of pure principles, and to give the immortal touch
of art to the names of our patriots and lawgivers.
Probably the latent spirit of the people is in this
respect in advance of the standard opinion of our
scholastic men and our men of wealth; and as
in the defence of the nation against treason, so in
its due elevation by the potent hand of art, our people will surprise the plodding world by their readiness to welcome every noble inspiration that gives
the country her due place among the nations and
owns her due loyalty to the kingdom of God. Our
people will appreciate Crawford's patriotic work
more and more, and Richmond, no longer estrangéd,
will in time be a shrine of pilgrimage to Northern

patriots who go thither to look upon the noblest of American monuments, with its statues of Washington and Patrick Henry and Jefferson and Marshall, that stand for the union and liberty that they won for the whole country.

This New York Historical Society has done its part in this direction, and will do it still.

You, Mr. President and gentlemen, have built this solid hall of remembrance and filled it with treasures of letters and art, and opened it to the young generation.

Nowhere in this land is there a better collection of historical memorials, and to-night a noble piece of sculpture is added to the wealth of canvas and marble that have long been gathering.

We have the requisite conditions for a great institution of history and the arts. There is none so good, nor is there likely to be any. Let the new building rise in its strength and beauty, with ample room for all the arts, for letters, sculpture, painting; all that presents the life of men and nations, and speaks to our children its august memories and its inspiring hopes. Here let our citizens present their august fellowship with the nations and the race, counting nothing human foreign to our blood. Here let our rich treasures unite their wealth and their witness. Here let the marbles of Nineveh and the antiquities of Egypt join with the art of Italy, Flanders, Holland, Spain, France, Germany, and our own land to enrich our American birthright, and to tell coming generations that we look to a worthy future, because we grow

3

from a substantial root in the past and feed upon
its unfailing spring of strength and beauty and joy.
Here write in letters and books, on canvas, in brass
and in marble, the Word of History, and God and
Humanity will breathe the Spirit of Life.

TRIBUTE TO CRAWFORD, DECEMBER 14, 1857.

The address is made more complete by recalling the commemorative discourse of Professor George W. Greene, December 14, 1857, and the remarks from Dr. Osgood that followed, which we here insert from the *Evening Post* of that week.

"The anniversary discourse of the New York Historical Society was given on Tuesday, December 14, by Prof. George W. Greene, of this city, and treated of the life and genius of Thomas Crawford, the gifted sculptor, whose sad death has taken from us perhaps the first of American artists. The discourse will be published. We add a few words of Rev. Dr. Osgood, who was asked to introduce the resolution of thanks.

"Dr. Osgood, after reading the resolution, said: "I am most happy, Mr. President, to express the thanks of the Society for the beautiful and eloquent address to which we have just listened, and cannot but think the subject most appropriate for the second anniversary in our new and expressive edifice. This building is dedicated to history, in the highest sense of the term, and includes art as well as letters, in its records of the deeds and thoughts of men. Our galleries of painting and sculpture, as well as our library and archives, preserve the mark of man upon the ages, and history, as we read it, is written with the sculptor's chisel and the painter's pencil quite as emphatically as by the author's pen and the printer's type. It is just, therefore, to give this anniversary evening to the memory of our great—probably our greatest—American sculptor, and our satisfaction in what we have heard to-night is as warrantable as it is unanimous.

"I do not profess to be an adept in the beautiful arts, whether of the connoisseur or the amateur kind, and am the more eneouraged to throw out a few thoughts suggested by the address, from the very fact that I speak somewhat as an outsider, and my words may have something of the same interest as the notes of a strange traveller—some Hindoo or Chinese—upon our land and people. The first thought that comes to me is the cheering conviction that kind Providence, in the ample bestowal of material goods and enterprise, does not evidently mean to stint us in respect to the rarer gifts of intellect and beauty, but is kindling on every side, in the spirits of chosen men of our people, the same divine fire that has glowed in the genius of a Phidias and Apelles, a Raphael and Michael Angelo. Education can do much, but it can never bring out of a man what God never put into him, and genius is born whilst knowledge is acquired. Education trained Crawford's hand to its skill, but God gave him his genius, and this obscure New York boy, whose labors we now honor, was taught of heaven before he was taught of men, that he belonged to the elect priesthood of the beautiful arts. His example, with that of not a few others, is therefore most cheering, and encourages us in the faith that whilst we are for a time obliged to rough it in this new country, and work hard for that prime essential, our bread and butter, in due season we shall carve arabesques upon the bread-plate, and embroider flowers into our table-cloth, and exalt our plodding utility by all the refinements of taste and creations of beauty. On every side artistic genius is developing itself, and proud as we are of our ploughs and reapers, our presses and engines, we have no reason to be ashamed either of our artists or their patrons, nor to doubt that this land of corn and cotton can bear its full proportion of herbs of grace and flowers of loveliness.

"This satisfaction in the promise of American art does not move us to the rabid kind of patriotism that scoffs at everything foreign, and, in its attempt to magnify, actually belittles us, by cutting us off from the Old World and making us a fragment of humanity instead of a hemisphere of the full globe. Crawford properly went to Rome to school his genius under the discipline of the best masters and to study the great works that treasure up the riches of all ages in those priceless repositories. It is well for us Americans thus to believe that we belong not to ourselves alone, but to humanity; and that as we receive much from the Old World, so we owe much, and are called to pay back our debt for so much wisdom and beauty by new enterprises of manliness and inspirations of hope. The fear is, however, that our youth who travel in Europe and revel in the arts of Italy, will refine their taste at the expense of their originality, if not soften their manners at the cost of their manhood. Most of them seem to weaken their force as they widen their range, and to come back enchanted rather than inspired. But enchantment is not inspiration. Calypso's grotto is not Apollo's temple, nor is Circe's cup Castalia's fountain. Crawford did not confound the two experiences nor lose his originality among the master-pieces of ancient art and the distortions of modern critics. Perhaps, without being conscious of it, he embodied his own brave thought upon the genius of Italy, that mausoleum of humanity, whose inspiration is a remembrance rather than a hope, in his marvellous statue of Orpheus, who is represented as' calling up, by the charm of his music, the spirits of the dead, instead of leading on the march of living humanity by his cheering strain. Italy, too, is looking, like Orpheus, into the under world, and, like him, vainly trying to recall its cherished past, that lost Eurydice. Italy, who gave Crawford the finishing touch of her skill, did not overlay his originality by her traditions. He turned from the land of Memory to the new world of Hope, and his Washington embodied his faith, whilst it crowned his genius.

"The statue at Richmond is Crawford's history of the Father of our Country, and it will be read for ages by eager eyes, under the light of God's own heaven, when most of the rhetoric that is now called immortal is forgotten, and the people who call him blessed shall fill the continent with their civilization and girdle the globe with their industry.

"There is something very friendly and sympathetic in the look of this great assembly here met in honor of a fellow-citizen whose brilliant life was full of trials, and whose early death was a tragedy of anguish and disappointment. He was more sadly afflicted than Milton, whose eyes,

> " So thick a drop severe hath quench'd their orbs,
> Or dim suffusion veiled."

" The poet's work may prosper without sight, and he may sing

> " As the wakeful bird
> Sings darkling, and, in shadiest covert hid,
> Tunes her nocturnal note."

" But how shall the sculptor guide his hand without that friendly light? The sense of vision—that gate called Beautiful to this living temple, the body—was to Crawford most painfully darkened and closed.   Yet to him the world of loveliness was not sealed up, for, under God's discipline, sight becomes insight, and the shapes of beauty that for years had been passing through that temple-gate were now kneeling before the interior shrine.   The Ideal that was the dream of his boyhood and the life of his maturity did not desert him in his dark sorrow, but was trans-figured into faith in the truth and beauty that are heavenly and eternal.   There is something in the genial and grateful spirit of this assembly that throws brightness over our artist's great sor-row and premature death, and brings him to us in his health and joy.   May we not devoutly trust that he who loyally gave himself to the chosen ministry of Beauty does not renounce the mind in putting off the body, nor abjure his ruling love in quitting its earthly sphere?   We leave his soul with that Infinite and Eternal Spirit whom we are called to know and adore, not only as the Almighty and All-Wise, but also as the All-Merciful and All-Lovely."

PROCEEDINGS OF THE SOCIETY.

At a stated meeting of the NEW YORK HISTORICAL SOCIETY, held in its Hall, on Tuesday evening, April 6th, 1875,

"The Librarian, Mr. MOORE, read a letter from the President, as follows :

"*Library of the New York Historical Society,*
April 6, 1875.

"GEORGE H. MOORE, LL.D., Librarian, &c.

"My dear Sir—Having purchased from Mrs. Louisa W. Terry, executrix of the last will and testament of the late Thomas Crawford, his marble statue of ' *The Indian,*' I now offer it as a gift to the New York Historical Society.

"The papers relating to its proper legal transfer are communicated herewith, as the muniments of title for the Society.

"I trust that this noble work, regarded as the masterpiece of its distinguished author, may remain in perpetuity among our collections, to commemorate the Indian of North America.

"FREDERIC DE PEYSTER,
"*President, &c.*"

The paper of the evening was then read by the Rev. Dr. SAMUEL OSGOOD, on "*Thomas Crawford and Art in America.*"

Mr. WILLIAM J. HOPPIN submitted the following resolutions, which were seconded by Mr. JOHN AUSTIN STEVENS, and adopted unanimously :

Resolved, That the thanks of the Society are cordially extended to our President, FREDERIC DE PEYSTER, for his munificent gift of the colossal statue of "*The Indian,*" by the eminent sculptor Thomas Crawford.

Resolved, That in our acknowledgment of this princely addition to our treasures, we recall the many previous similar benefactions, as well in works of literature as of art, with which Mr. DE PEYSTER has enriched the collections of the Society.

Resolved, That we recognize with pleasure in this grateful record the names of two so highly honored sons of New York—the Artist and the Citizen—now forever united by grateful association in the thoughts and affections of our members.

*　　*　　*　　*　　*　　*　　*

Mr. ERASTUS C. BENEDICT submitted the following resolution, which was seconded by Mr. JAMES H. TITUS, and adopted unanimously:

Resolved, That the thanks of the Society be presented to the Rev. SAMUEL OSGOOD, for his able and eloquent paper read this evening, and that a copy be requested for publication."

Extract from the Minutes.

ANDREW WARNER,
Recording Secretary.

www.ingramcontent.com/pod-product-compliance
Lightning Source LLC
Chambersburg PA
CBHW030913260626